VICTORIA

BY

JOHN GUY

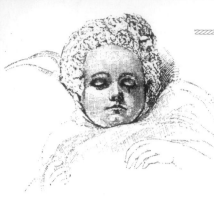

THE YOUNG VICTORIA

Victoria was born at Kensington Palace and was christened exactly one month later in the Cupola Room at the Palace. There was a dispute over her name, her parents eventually settling on Alexandrina Victoria as her registered name, but they called her Victoria from birth.

*W*hen Victoria was born on 24 May 1819 she was fifth in line to the throne and the likelihood of her succeeding seemed very remote. Her grandfather, George III, was still king and ahead of her in succession were her uncles, George, the Prince Regent, the Dukes of York and Clarence, and of course her father, the Duke of Kent. Within a short space of time, however, all that changed. Her father died unexpectedly on 23 January 1820 followed, six days later, by her grandfather. The Duke of York died in 1827, taking her a step nearer the throne. Her remaining uncles succeeded as George IV and William IV, respectively, but their failing health produced no heirs, leaving Victoria as heir to the throne.

PERSONAL POSSESSIONS

Many of Queen Victoria's personal possessions still survive, a number of them on view at the Victoria and Albert Museum. These reading glasses once belonged to the Queen; the case is inscribed with her personal insignia.

WILLIAM IV

Victoria's uncle, William IV, became King at the age of 64 on the death of his brother, and when he died in 1837 he left no legitimate heirs to the throne. Victoria became queen as his closest living relative.

THE YOUNG PRINCESS

Always a friendly and playful child (who had no fewer than 132 dolls!), she had an aptitude for music, singing and dancing and was an accomplished artist. She spoke with a strong German accent as a child, because of her mother's German origins, and she could speak German and French fluently.

THE QUEEN COMES OF AGE

Princess Victoria was just 18 years old when she heard of the death of her uncle, William IV, in 1837. She was immediately filled with feelings of both happiness and sadness, but seems to have assumed the awesome responsibility with apparent calm. She was crowned the following year, on 28 June, at Westminster Abbey. Not a popular figure at first, she was destined to become Britain's longest reigning monarch and ruler over the greatest empire the world has ever seen.

DUCHESS OF KENT

Victoria's father was Edward, Duke of Kent, fourth son of George III. Victoria never knew her father, who died when she was a baby. Her mother, the Duchess of Kent, was appointed Regent in case Victoria succeeded to the throne whilst still a child.

PRINCE ALBERT

One of the first dilemmas facing Victoria when she succeeded to the throne was that of marriage. Lord Melbourne, the Prime Minister, advised Victoria to marry as soon as possible to create her own heirs. At first she had no interest in doing so but agreed to meet her cousin, Prince Albert of Saxe-Coburg-Gotha. Both entered the relationship reluctantly at first, but there seems to have been a mutual attraction and they soon became very dear friends. After marriage their friendship developed into a very deep and genuine love for one another and they became a devoted couple.

THE PRINCE CONSORT

Prince Albert was, in Victoria's own words, *'so sensible, so kind, and so good, and so amiable…the most pleasing and delightful exterior and appearance you can possibly see.'* He was tall, intelligent and proved to be a very able political adviser to Victoria. He took a genuine interest in his new adoptive country, particularly the poorer classes. He is credited with re-introducing the practice of bringing decorated Christmas trees into the house, a custom still practised in his native Germany, though it had long fallen out of favour in England.

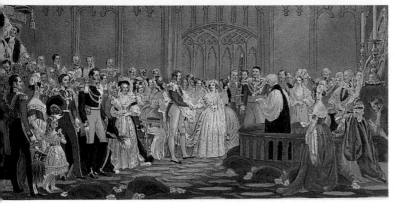

THE ROYAL WEDDING

The wedding between Victoria and Albert took place on 10 February 1840 at St. James's Palace. They were both just 20 years old. She wore a white satin gown with a lace flounce, and a Turkish diamond necklace and sapphire brooch (a present from Albert). The couple were well received by the public. After the wedding reception held at Buckingham Palace, they had a three-day honeymoon at Windsor Castle.

THE PRINCE DIES

In 1861 Prince Albert contracted typhoid and died prematurely, at the age of 42. The Queen was heartbroken. The prospect of facing the world alone culminated in a nervous breakdown. She wore black for the rest of her life in respect for Albert. At first the public sympathized with her, but after over a decade of mourning, there were calls for her abdication.

THE QUEEN PROPOSES

According to the dictates of royal protocol, no man is allowed to propose to a queen, so Victoria had to ask for Albert's hand in marriage. She proposed to him on 15 October 1839. In her diary, Victoria wrote that Albert's acceptance was the brightest and happiest moment of her life.

KEEPSAKES

To commemorate the royal wedding a great many mementoes were made, such as this decorative lustre-ware jug.

EVENTS OF VICTORIA'S LIFE

~1819~
Victoria born at Kensington Palace

~1820~
Victoria's father Edward, Duke of Kent, dies

~1830~
George IV dies

William IV accedes to the throne

~1832~
First Reform Act passed to reform parliamentary system

~1833~
Slavery abolished throughout the Empire

~1834~
Poor Law creates workhouses for the poor

Houses of Parliament burn down

~1837~
William IV dies

Victoria accedes to the throne

~1838~
Victoria's coronation

People's Charter issued, calling for political reform

~1839~
First camera developed

~1840~
Victoria marries Albert of Saxe-Coburg-Gotha

FAMILY LIFE

*V*ictoria is often pictured as a stern, austere woman, an image perpetuated by her choice to wear black for so many years after Albert's death. She is seldom seen smiling in pictures, but supposedly was a jovial person. One reason for her glum expressions was possibly the slow film speed used by photographers at the time. Subjects often had to hold a pose for 30 seconds (or longer) so as not to blur the image, making it difficult to hold a smile. Historians have often concentrated on the more serious side to Victoria's personality, neglecting her love of life, particularly family life. She was amused by the antics of children and both she and Albert enjoyed simple, family pastimes. In later life, Victoria loved to see herself as the great matriarch.

SOFTLY, SOFTLY

Contrary to popular opinion, Victoria was not a strict authoritarian. She preferred to instruct her children by setting a good moral example rather than to over-discipline them.

THE GRANDMOTHER OF EUROPE

This picture, taken in 1897, shows the extended family of Queen Victoria. The Prince of Wales (and future king Edward VII) stands immediately to her left. By the various marriages of her children and grand-children, Victoria was related to all of the major royal houses of Europe, including Germany, Norway, Sweden, Greece, Spain, Romania and Russia, earning her the affectionate title 'the grandmother of Europe'.

HAPPY FAMILIES

In keeping with most families of the day, Victoria and Albert had many children, nine in all. She gave birth to Princess Victoria (Vicky) in November 1840. Vicky, the Princess Royal, remained a close friend throughout the Queen's life, especially after Albert's death. Victoria's family life was, by all accounts, a happy one. It is difficult to say what kind of relationship she had with all her children: some accounts claim she was aloof and dispassionate, others paint a rosier picture. There does appear to have been real animosity between her and Edward, the future king, whom she thought foolish, and was critical of his behaviour.

PERSONAL RECOLLECTIONS

We know a great deal about the personal life and opinions of Queen Victoria from her diary, which she maintained throughout her life. It was not, as many suppose, a secret diary, certainly not in her younger years, because it was frequently perused by her mother and governess.

~1840~
Penny postal service introduced

Princess 'Vicky' born (Victoria's first child)

~1841~
Sir Robert Peel becomes Prime Minister

~1845~
Beginning of Irish potato famine

~1846~
Corn Laws repealed

~1851~
Great Exhibition in London, initiated by Prince Albert

~1853~
Vaccination against smallpox made compulsory

Albert begins rebuilding Balmoral Castle to his own designs

~1854~
Crimean War breaks out between Britain (and France) and Russia

~1856~
Victoria Cross first introduced for bravery in wartime

~1857~
Indian Mutiny against British rule

ASSASSINATION ATTEMPTS

At the beginning of her reign Victoria was not a popular figure at all. As ruling monarch, she was often seen as the cause of social discontent; some would have preferred a king on the throne. There were several attempts made on Victoria's life including this attempt in 1840 by Edward Oxford.

REFORM ACTS

During her reign, Victoria approved several Acts of Parliament that had important social and constitutional implications. Growing unrest in Britain meant new political movements were forcing change. In 1838 the Chartists issued the 'Peoples' Charter' which called for political reform. Although not fully realized until 1944, it forms the basis of our parliamentary system today. In 1867 and 1884, the Second and Third Reform Acts extended the right to vote to more people.

FATHER FIGURE

During the early years of her reign Victoria relied heavily on the advice of Lord Melbourne, the Whig (Liberal) Prime Minister, who guided her through the intricacies of politics and her role in government.

SOCIAL CHANGE

The Industrial Revolution saw Britain change from a mainly agricultural nation to an industrial one. People who left the country to seek employment in the towns were exploited by greedy industrialists. Trade unionists like Joseph Arch, founder of the National Union of Farm Labourers (shown right), fought a long and hard battle for workers' rights. Trade unions were finally legalized in 1871.

VICTORIA & GOVERNMENT

From the beginning Victoria showed a genuine interest in the government of the country and developed a good rapport with most of the leading politicians of the day. She took her role seriously and, whilst accepting the relatively new idea of a constitutional monarchy (which meant that she had no real part to play in politics), she also realized that she had considerable influence and exercised her powers wisely. Albert, who had shown little interest in politics prior to their marriage, also took an active role in matters of government.

POLITICAL GIANTS

Victoria witnessed the coming and going of several great politicians, including William Gladstone and Benjamin Disraeli. Victoria liked Disraeli (above) and had him invested Earl of Beaconsfield, whereas Gladstone frequently incurred her wrath.

A NEW HOUSE FOR PARLIAMENT

Until the reign of Victoria's uncle, William IV, Parliament met in the old royal palace of Westminster. Like most medieval buildings, it contained a lot of wood and burned down in a disastrous fire in 1834. The present Houses of Parliament were rebuilt on part of the old palace site. Victoria officiated at the opening of the new building in 1867.

LIFE EXPECTANCY

This picture shows a father comforting his dying child. Childhood deaths were not uncommon in Victorian Britain. There was no National Health Service and the poor could rarely afford medical treatment. In the country the life expectancy was around 50, but for those living in squalid conditions in towns many were lucky to reach 40.

SMALLPOX

One of the most contagious and deadly diseases was smallpox. The scientist, Edward Jenner, pioneered a vaccine to combat the disease. Vaccination was made compulsory in 1853.

SANITATION

Many of the diseases prevalent in Victorian Britain were caused through poor sanitation and living conditions. A series of Public Health Acts after 1848 made it the responsibility of local councils to provide proper drainage and clean water supplies. Only the rich could afford the luxury of an indoor toilet. The poor had to make do with open cesspits in the backyard or, worse still, a communal toilet shared by up to 100 others.

LIFE IN VICTORIAN ENGLAND

*A*t the beginning of Victoria's reign (1837), the population of Britain was about 20 million, only 20 per cent of whom lived in towns. The rest still managed to eke out a living from the land. By the end of her reign (1901) the population had doubled with over 75 per cent living in towns. These burgeoning populations meant that row upon row of poor-quality terraced slums were erected around the factories. Living conditions were appalling and disease was rife, particularly water-borne diseases such as cholera and typhoid.

POSTAL SERVICE

No proper postal service had existed in Britain until 1840 when the Penny Post was introduced. This revolutionized the delivery of letters and for just 1d. (0.4p) a letter could be sent anywhere in the country. The first stamp issued was the Penny Black. It carried a profile of the Queen, a tradition adopted throughout the Empire and still maintained today.

WORK ETHIC

Workhouses were first introduced in 1834 and were often the only help available for the poor and homeless in Victorian towns. People received basic food and lodging in return for work, often in extremely harsh conditions.

SOCIAL HISTORIAN

Charles Dickens (1812-70) was the greatest and most popular novelist of his day. Many of his novels, such as *Oliver Twist*, paint a vivid description of life in Victorian Britain and he was often regarded as a champion of the poor.
Victoria started to accept Dickens's picture of Britain when her own beloved husband died of typhoid, contracted most probably from the open sewers around Windsor.

11

ART & INVENTIONS

ART FOR ART'S SAKE

Both Victoria and Charles Dickens spoke out against the Pre-Raphaelite movement in art. The Pre-Raphaelites were a brotherhood of young artists (including Millais, whose *The Bridesmaid* is shown here) who rejected the artistic 'establishment' and classical themes.

The speed at which new inventions and discoveries appeared in Victorian Britain was phenomenal. These developments changed the way people had been living almost overnight. The first electric light bulbs were invented in America by Thomas Edison who, in 1877, also invented the phonograph (forerunner of modern hi-fi). The telephone was invented in 1875 by another American, Alexander Graham Bell. Food processing and packaging in tins kept food fresh for longer. Many items, however, were still relatively expensive and so were enjoyed only by the wealthy.

PHOTOGRAPHIC RECORD

Victoria's was the first reign in history to be fully documented in photographs. The first primitive photographic images were produced in 1800. The first camera, as shown here, was developed by William Fox Talbot in 1839.

THE MEDICINE MEN

The Victorian Age was one of great learning, a period when great minds collaborated to push the bounds of human knowledge to the limits. Doctors such as Joseph Lister recognized that bacteria were the cause of infection. He developed an antiseptic in 1867. Prior to that, chloroform had been developed for use as an anaesthetic during operations. Victoria herself was administered chloroform during the birth of her last child, Beatrice, in 1857.

ARTISTIC LICENCE

It has often been said that the Victorians did not have an architectural style of their own, but merely borrowed from past eras. In fact, their use of cast iron and glass is a style wholly their own. In more traditional buildings they freely interpreted a variety of styles, such as medieval, to create 'Victorian Gothick', as seen here at Cardiff Castle.

GRANDIOSE IDEAS

The Victorians built on a monumental scale. They erected the largest buildings then known, reflecting the bold confidence of the new industrial age. The use of cast iron and glass made it possible to span huge floor areas. This view shows the railway station at St. Pancras under construction.

AGE OF SCIENCE

Michael Faraday's experiments with electro-magnetism realized the full potential of electricity as a major power source. Eager to promote the use of new technologies, Queen Victoria had electric lighting installed in all her palaces. She also demonstrated this new technology during her Diamond Jubilee celebrations in 1897 by pressing an electric button that was connected to a telegraph. It transmitted a message throughout the Empire, beginning the tradition of the royal broadcast on Christmas Day.

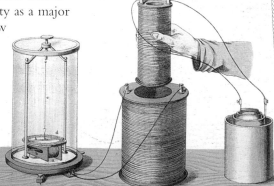

EVENTS OF VICTORIA'S LIFE

~1859~
Charles Darwin publishes
Origin of the Species

~1861~
Prince Albert dies
of typhoid

Victoria goes into
mourning and withdraws
from public life

~1863~
Edward, Prince of Wales
(Victoria's eldest son and
heir) marries Alexandra
of Denmark

~1867~
Canada becomes first
country within British
Empire to be declared
an independent
dominion

Second Reform
Bill passed; further
parliamentary reforms

New Houses of
Parliament opened

~1868~
Gladstone becomes
Prime Minister

THE GREAT EXHIBITION

JOSEPH PAXTON

The Crystal Palace building was designed by Joseph Paxton, a brilliant engineer who had erected huge conservatories at stately homes, but this was his masterpiece. It was truly a wonder of the age and prompted Queen Victoria to call it a 'fairy-tale palace'. Paxton received the fee of £5,000 (which is the equivalent of £1 million today) for designing and building it.

The Great Exhibition of 1851 was the brainchild of Prince Albert. He believed that an international exhibition in London would both act as a shop window for British industry and generate more work to benefit the poor. His ideas were not met with enthusiasm by the government but, undaunted, he won popular support and private finance through the press. The exhibition was opened on 1 May 1851 by Queen Victoria and was a resounding success. From then, until its closure on 15 October, over six million people visited the exhibition at a time when Britain's population was only about 20 million. It was the first international trade exhibition in the world.

PREFABRICATED BUILDING

The Crystal Palace, shown here during its original construction, was made of prefabricated parts which enabled the building to be taken down after the exhibition closed in Hyde Park and re-erected some miles away at Sydenham in 1854. The area is still known as Crystal Palace. Sadly, the building burned down in a disastrous fire in 1936.

FROM FAR AND WIDE

Inside the exhibition building there were over 14,000 different exhibitors, over half of whom were from the British Empire. Industrialists from across the globe came to view the best of British industry and place orders for all manner of commodities, from steam trains to spinning machines, textiles to fine art. Admission charges were reduced after two days to ensure that people of all classes could attend.

MUSEUMS FOR ALL

Albert determined that the ordinary people of Britain should benefit from the exhibition; money raised from the proceeds was used to open several large museums in London. These included the Victoria and Albert, the Science and the Natural History Museums, which collectively became the envy of the world.

THE CRYSTAL PALACE

The original exhibition building, erected at Hyde Park, was a masterpiece of cast iron and glass, earning it the title 'The Crystal Palace'. It covered an area of 26 acres and was three times the size of St. Paul's Cathedral. It was about 550 metres (600 yards) long and contained over 300,000 individual panes of glass.

WORKSHOP OF THE WORLD

MAN OF GENIUS

Throughout the Victorian era there were men of exceptional genius and vision. Isambard Kingdom Brunel was such a man. A brilliant and innovative engineer, he specialized in the use of iron and steel in his designs for ships and civil engineering projects. His revolutionary liner, the *Great Britain,* was launched by Prince Albert in 1843; the biggest ship ever built.

*T*he Victorians believed that work was a virtue and was good for the soul – none more than Victoria herself, whose own workload was quite prodigious. Technological developments were faster in Britain than anywhere else in the world. Britain had been the first to embrace the new 'industrial revolution' sweeping the developed countries, earning it the title 'Workshop of the World'.

WORKING CONDITIONS

The working class bore the brunt of the rapid industrialization. People used to rural outdoor life now had to work in mines and factories, often some distance away from their homes and in cramped and airless conditions.

THE PRICE OF PROGRESS

One of the worst aspects of town life was the pollution that resulted from burning large quantities of fossil fuels, such as coal. Victoria increasingly found life in London intolerable and spent long periods in the country.

CHILD LABOUR

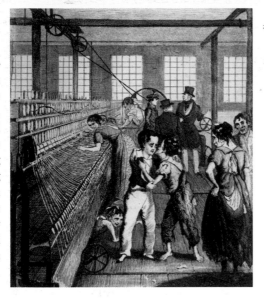

Women and children were used to working on farms, but in industrial Britain they were forced to work long hours in appalling conditions. Fourteen hours a day was quite usual and factory owners would employ children as young as five.

WHEEL OF FORTUNE

The industrialization of Britain and the strength of the Empire were of mutual benefit. The new industries sold their products to the colonies, and in turn, the colonies supplied Britain with endless raw materials to make yet more goods. So the cycle continued. A large merchant fleet was essential for the transportation of these goods, and Britain had the largest navy to protect the merchant ships.

RAILWAYS

At the beginning of Victoria's reign there were about 3,200 kilometres (2,000 miles) of railway in Britain. By 1870 this figure had grown to 22,000 kilometres (13,750 miles). At first there was strong resistance to railways, especially from canal owners, but 'railway mania' soon erupted. Branch lines opened up all over the country, transporting goods cheaply and quickly from the factories to the ports.

FIRST COLONIES

The British Empire began as a small collection of colonies along the eastern coast of North America. They formed themselves into 13 states, and gained their independence in the reign of Victoria's grandfather, George III. Colonies were also established in what is now Canada during a search for a north-west passage to Asia.

THE MILITARY

Although Britain's Empire was not primarily military led, countries subjected to British rule were held down by a strong military presence.

THE INDIAN MUTINY

Since the 18th century, the East India Company had employed Indian troops. In 1857, these native troops rebelled and a series of bloody battles ensued. The mutiny was eventually crushed and India came under the direct rule of the British Government. In 1876, Victoria became Empress of India, a title all future monarchs retained until India received its independence in 1947.

THE EAST INDIA COMPANY

Elizabethan mariners first landed in India in the 16th century, opening a number of trade routes. In 1600, the East India Company was set up to protect British interests in India and develop further trading contacts with Asia.

THE BRITISH EMPIRE . . .

By the end of Victoria's reign she presided over the largest empire that the world had ever seen. Always conscious of her position as its monarchical head, Victoria was greatly responsible for creating the 'family of nations', later known as the Commonwealth. Unlike other past empires, the interests of the British Empire lay with trade and the wealth it generated, rather than world domination. Although aided by the military, it was not military led, and colonies were acquired in a piecemeal fashion, stretching across the globe.

ORIGINS OF THE EMPIRE

The origins of the British Empire can be traced to the reign of Elizabeth I. In Elizabeth's time, England was often at war with other European nations, particularly Spain who controlled all the major trade routes to the Americas and the East. A series of voyages to uncharted areas of the world became quests for new trade routes and land to establish new colonies.

ROBERT CLIVE

Britain's rule in India began with the victory of Robert Clive in 1757. He defeated the massive combined Indo–French army of 60,000 with a small force of 3,000 men, securing the province of Bengal. Although regarded as a hero back in Britain, Clive was understandably hated by the Indians.

EXTENT OF THE EMPIRE

This map shows the extent of the British Empire (coloured orange) in 1886. All of the major trading routes were under British control, which explains why Britain was such a major influence throughout the world.

BRITISH WAY OF LIFE

When subjugating a new land, the British forced the native people to adopt British ways. Official buildings and houses were built in British styles and British legal and government systems were introduced. The English language became widely-spoken and remains the most dominant language in the world.

EQUAL PORTIONS

Throughout the 18th and 19th centuries there was considerable land-hunger amongst the major world powers. They had the attitude that the world was theirs for the taking and had little regard for the native peoples. This cartoon shows various heads of state dividing up China like a piece of pie, while the Chinese leader looks on helplessly.

THE BRITISH EMPIRE . . .

The British Empire grew slowly. At its fullest extent it covered one quarter of the world's land mass. It reached its zenith immediately after the First World War, when the former German colonies in Africa and Asia were taken over. Because its colonies were scattered across the globe, resources were eventually stretched too thinly. The military were unable to cope and when Britain began to have economic problems at home, the Empire gradually went into decline.

FLYING THE FLAG

The raising of the Union Jack to denote British sovereignty over a newly acquired country was always treated with a great deal of reverence, accompanied by much pomp and ceremony.

VOYAGES OF DISCOVERY

In Elizabethan times, the motives for exploration were quite simple: gold and new trade routes. By Victoria's reign, it was commonplace for explorers to take scientists with them on their voyages, to record and bring back samples of new plants and animal species for scientific study. This practice was started by explorers such as James Cook who is seen here raising the Union Jack in New South Wales, Australia, in 1770.

THE BRITISH EMPIRE

"NEW CROWNS FOR OLD ONES!"

EMPRESS OF INDIA

In 1876 Queen Victoria was proclaimed Empress of India and was proud to accept the title. She is seen here, in this contemporary cartoon, being asked by Prime Minister Disraeli to trade the imperial crown of India for her own.

The reign of Victoria was a golden era, a time when even the Queen herself believed that the 'sun would never set on the Empire'. It coincided with a period of great social and economic change, when Britain led the world in science and technology. Although the British government exploited the colonies, many of them benefited from Britain's developments. Many of the world's railway systems, for example, were built by British engineers, and commodities made in Britain were exported all over the globe. In short, Britain took the world by storm.

FRESH START

One of the strengths of the British Empire lay in colonizing subjugated nations with British citizens. Like these emigrants bound for Sydney, many were keen to try a fresh start in the colonies, faced with poverty and unemployment at home.

THE GERMAN THREAT

The main threat to the Empire came, not from rebelling colonies, but from Germany; more specifically from Victoria's own grandson, Kaiser Wilhelm II. Although Britain's navy was by far the greatest in the world, Germany was able to build warships of the very latest design at a faster rate than Britain could replace its obsolete ones.

BRITANNIA RULES THE WAVES

Four days after Victoria's Diamond Jubilee, in 1897, the Royal Navy staged a massive display of its power at Spithead, on the south coast. It was the largest collection of warships ever assembled and demonstrated to the world the might of the British Empire.

SLAVERY ABOLISHED

Slavery was abolished throughout the Empire in 1833, some years before Victoria's reign. The treatment of native peoples from the colonies was a matter close to the Queen's heart. She strongly resisted giving the Boers of South Africa their independence, for example, fearing they would treat the natives too harshly.

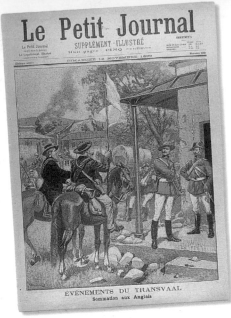

ÉVÉNEMENTS DU TRANSVAAL
Sommation aux Anglais

BRITAIN AT WAR

Throughout Victoria's reign, as Britain greatly extended its empire, there were a number of imperial conflicts. With rising unemployment at home, there was no shortage of manpower to join the ranks of the army. Like Britain, all the other major powers in Europe were keen to acquire new colonies. This jostling for supremacy and land was the cause of one of the worst conflicts in history: the First World War.

BADEN-POWELL

The flamboyant Lieutenant-Colonel, Robert Baden-Powell, became a national hero during the Boer War. He made the small South African trading post of Mafeking his military headquarters and held the town, against 8,000 Boers, with just 1,000 soldiers, losing only 35 men. Baden-Powell went on to form the Boy Scout movement in 1908.

THE BOER WAR (1899-1902)

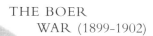

The Boers were South African farmers (descended from Dutch settlers) who fiercely resisted Britain's attempts to annexe South Africa after the discovery of gold there. They used guerrilla tactics to combat the massive British force sent against them, but eventually the sheer size of the British army crushed their resistance.

JOHN BERRYMAN, (TROOP SERG. MAJOR) REFUSING TO LEAVE CAPTAIN WEBB AT BALAKLAVA.

JOHN GREIVE (SERG. MAJOR) SAVING THE LIFE OF AN O. BALAKLAVA.

C. H. LUMLEY (BREVET MAJOR) IN THE REDAN, ENGAGED RUSSIAN GUNNERS.

THE CRIMEAN WAR (1854-56)

The Crimean War was fought between Britain and Russia on a peninsula that is now part of modern-day Turkey. Britain was unprepared for the scale of the conflict and suffered one of its worst military disasters, the 'Charge of the Light Brigade', at Balaclava in 1854.

FLORENCE NIGHTINGALE

Florence Nightingale (the 'Lady of the Lamp') is best remembered for her work in the Crimean War, tending to the injuries of wounded soldiers. Her reports of the horrors of the Crimea sent shock waves that were felt throughout society. Afterwards, she devoted her life to the better training of nurses.

THE VICTORIA CROSS

During the Crimean War, Victoria had a special medal struck for those who had served in the war. She insisted that no distinction be made between officers and privates – a revolutionary step for the day. She later created the Victoria Cross which is still the highest military honour accorded today.

THE ROYAL PALACES

V ictoria and Albert made full use of the royal palaces. For official duties, balls and government functions they favoured Buckingham Palace (shown here in 1852), but the Queen always preferred the privacy of Windsor Castle. As a young girl Victoria enjoyed the hurly-burly of London's social scene, but Albert was a country man at heart, preferring the peace and solitude of the country estates. Later in life, Victoria also came to prefer them.

BUCKINGHAM PALACE

The population census of 1841 shows Buckingham Palace to be Queen Victoria's main residence. It is still the residence most often associated with British royalty but is a relative newcomer to the list of royal palaces. Victoria's grandfather, George III, purchased the house for £28,000 in 1762. The state apartments are magnificent, and frequently host state functions.

OSBORNE HOUSE

In 1844, Victoria and Albert began looking for a house to which they could retire from the hustle and bustle of court life. The Osborne estate on the Isle of Wight proved ideal, and Prince Albert designed and built a new house in Italian Renaissance style.

BALMORAL CASTLE

This view shows part of Victoria's private apartments (the drawing room) at Balmoral Castle in Aberdeenshire. Surrounded by mountains and set in 30,000 acres of deer forest, Balmoral has always been a royal favourite since it was purchased and redesigned by Prince Albert in 1853.

WINDSOR CASTLE

Windsor Castle is the oldest royal residence in Britain and also the largest inhabited castle in the world. Begun by William the Conqueror in 1066 it has been greatly extended since then. Successive monarchs, right up to George IV, Victoria's uncle, continued the process of transforming the great medieval castle into a magnificent palace.

THE JUBILEE YEARS

*T*he last years of Victoria's reign were a marked contrast to the early years. Although she eventually came out of mourning for Albert some 13 years after his death (in 1874), she never got over his loss. She returned to public life, but with advancing years the queen became a sadder, more melancholic person. Victoria had not been universally popular throughout her reign. Many had not welcomed her to the throne, but by the time of her Golden Jubilee in 1887 she was at the height of her popularity.

NEVER-TO-BE-FORGOTTEN DAY

The Queen's Golden Jubilee marked 50 years of her reign. People throughout the Empire celebrated the event, particularly in Britain itself (and more especially in London) with wild enthusiasm. Victoria said of the occasion: '*This never-to-be-forgotten day will always leave the most gratifying and heart-stirring memories behind.*'

FAMILY GATHERING

On the occasion of her Golden Jubilee, Victoria attended a banquet held in her honour in Buckingham Palace. Invited guests included all the crowned heads of Europe, most of whom were related to Victoria. For her Diamond Jubilee in 1897, as this portrait shows, the gathering was of her 'extended family' and colonial premiers from countries throughout the Empire.

THE DIAMOND JUBILEE

This painting shows Queen Victoria arriving at St. Paul's Cathedral for a thanksgiving service on 22 June 1897, held in honour of her Diamond Jubilee. Out of respect for her age and ailing health the service was kept deliberately short.

ROYAL INVITE

This picture shows one of the formal invitations to the Queen's Diamond Jubilee celebrations at the Guildhall in London, one of many public functions held throughout the country. By this time the Queen was a frail old lady with bad rheumatism and failing eyesight, confined to a wheelchair. However, she continued to perform her duties right up until a few weeks before she died.

THE END OF AN ERA

FAMILY FEUDS

This family tree shows that most of Victoria's children married into the royal houses of Europe, which she hoped would have a stabilizing effect on European politics. Sadly, this was not to be.

*W*ith the death of Victoria on 22 January 1901, it really was the end of an era. In some respects Victoria was liberal in her attitude, taking a keen interest in improving the living conditions of the poor, but in other ways she was very conservative. She frowned upon the idea of women holding professions, yet she objected strongly to the working conditions imposed on women and children in the mines and factories. Similarly, she opposed giving the vote to women, but supported giving the vote to working class men. Britain had seen more change during her reign than in any other period in history, but the world was now poised on the threshold of a whole new age.

THREAT TO PEACE

This picture shows the Kaiser, William II, Victoria's grandson by the marriage of her daughter Vicky to Prince Frederick of Prussia. Victoria always resented his anti-British views, but he was at her bedside when she lay dying. Had she lived a few more years she would have seen him lead Germany against Britain in the First World War.

PROBLEM CHILD

This view shows Victoria with her son, the future King Edward VII, shortly before her death. She was always critical of Edward and did not feel he had the necessary qualities to make a good king. She deliberately kept him out of government issues for fear his head-strong attitude might create problems. In later life she finally acknowledged him as her heir.

TRUSTED ADVISER

Victoria followed a high moral code in life, but she was no stranger to scandal. During her period of mourning for Albert she befriended a Scots servant called John Brown, an excellent horseman, who the Queen trusted and took into her confidence. He became her constant companion and rumours began to circulate they were having an affair, causing her popularity to sink to an all-time low.

EVENTS OF VICTORIA'S LIFE

~1887~
Independent Labour Party founded

~1897~
Victoria's Diamond Jubilee celebrates 60 years on the throne

Spithead naval review

~1899~
Boer War breaks out in South Africa

~1900~
Victoria's son, Alfred, dies

~1901~
Queen Victoria dies; our longest reigning monarch

Edward VII accedes to the throne

FAMILY PORTRAIT

This family portrait was taken at Osborne House in 1898, three years before Victoria's death. When she died, her body was taken from there to Cowes and on to London. Her funeral was carried out according to her own instructions and she was buried at Frogmore, sharing the same mausoleum as her beloved husband, Prince Albert.

DID YOU KNOW?

That until Victoria's reign only the rich could afford to drink tea? Although it seems difficult to believe now, the humble cup of tea, the most popular drink in Britain today, used to be a luxury that few could afford. When the Empire expanded, tea was imported in bulk, from India and China, making it affordable by all classes for the first time.

That the Scouts movement had its origins in the Boer War? In 1908 Robert Baden-Powell published a small pamphlet entitled *Scouting for Boys*. It marked the beginnings of the scouting movement and soon boys were queuing up to join, attracted by the exciting world of adventure, camping and outdoor activities described in the booklet. Baden-Powell based many of the scouts activities directly on army life in South Africa, even copying the uniform from that worn by the military in hot climates.

That Charles Darwin suffered public derision and ill-health as a result of publishing his book *The Origin of the Species*? When Charles Darwin first published his famous book on evolution (on which most modern thought on evolution is derived) in 1859, there was a public outcry. Until then, many people believed in the literal truth of the Old Testament, especially the account of God's creation of the Earth. Darwin's revolutionary theories of natural selection were publicly criticized and he was accused of blasphemy by fellow scholars and eminent churchmen. Darwin was forced to challenge his own religious beliefs and was so overcome with guilt at daring to call into question Biblical authority that he became physically ill.

That the Brontë sisters adopted male names to avoid prejudice against women? The three Brontë sisters, Charlotte, Emily and Anne, amongst the most celebrated of Victorian novelists, were forced to use male pseudonyms in order to get their work published. They used the names Currer, Acton and Ellis Bell, respectively. The Brontës lonely life on the Yorkshire moors is reflected in their haunting novels, particularly Charlotte's *Jane Eyre* and Emily's *Wuthering Heights*. They all died within seven years of one another, all at very young ages.

That Railway timetables provided the first 'standard' time throughout Britain? Prior to the expansion of the railway system in Victorian times, people in Britain set their clocks by the position of the sun. This meant that clocks in the far west of the country showed a slightly different time to those in the east. This made it difficult for train drivers and signalmen, who needed to know the precise time of a train's arrival. A standard 'railway time', based on Greenwich meantime in London, was introduced at all railway stations and this eventually became accepted by everyone across the country as 'standard time'.

ACKNOWLEDGEMENTS

We would like to thank: Graham Rich, Rosalind Beckman and Elizabeth Wiggans for their assistance.

Copyright © 1998 ticktock Publishing Ltd.

First published in Great Britain by ticktock Publishing Ltd., The Offices in the Square, Hadlow, Tonbridge, Kent, TN11 0DD. All rights reserved. No part of this publication may be reproduced, stored in a retrieval system, or transmitted in any form or by any means electronic, mechanical, photocopying, recording or otherwise, without prior written permission of the copyright owner.

A CIP catalogue record for this book is available from the British Library. ISBN 1 86007 033 7

Picture research by Image Select.

Printed in Italy.

Picture Credits:
t=top, b=bottom, c=centre, l=left, r=right, OFC=outside front cover, IFC=inside front cover, OBC=outside back cover, IBC=inside back cover

Ann Ronan at Image Select International Ltd; OBC - right, 2tl, 2br, 4r, 5c, 6bl, 6tl, 8tr, 8c, 9tr, 9bl & OFC, 10bl & OBC, 10br, 10t, 11br, 11tr & OBC, 12bl, 13br, 13c, 14tl, 14bl, 16br, 16tl & OBC, 16/17c & OFC, 17t, 17br, 18l, 18/19c, 19tr, 21b, 22b, 22tl, 23tl, 23tr, 24bl, 24/25cb, 25cr & 25br, 30tl, 31tr. The Bridgeman Art Library, London; OBC - bottom left, 3br, 3tl, 3t, 4l & OFC, 5bl, 7tl, 8bl, 11cb, 12tl, 13tl, 15tl, 16bl, 18/19cb, 20t, 20bl, 23bl & 23br, 26/27 (main image), 27tr, 28bl & OFC (main image), 28tl & OFC, 29cl, 30/31c. Bridgeman - Giraudon; IFC & 29tr. Chris Fairclough Colour Library at Image Select International Ltd; 9br, 27c. The Fotomas Index (London); 2bl, 6/7cb, 19br. By Courtesy of Fine Art Photographic Library; 25t. Image Select International Ltd; 12/13c, 14/15c, 18tr,, 26tl, 30/31cb, 30bl. Mary Evans Picture Library, London; 5tl, 15br, 20br & OFC, 24tl, 32c & OFC, 26/27c, 29b. Spectrum Colour Library; 21tr.

Every effort has been made to trace the copyright holders and we apologize in advance for any unintentional omissions. We would be pleased to insert the appropriate acknowledgement in any subsequent edition of this publication.

snapping-turtle guide